Student Note-Taking Guide to ac

Nutrition

Second Edition

Paul Insel

R. Elaine Turner

Don Ross

JONES AND BARTLETT PUBLISHERS

Sudbury, Massachusetts

BOSTON   TORONTO   LONDON   SINGAPORE

World Headquarters
Jones and Bartlett Publishers
40 Tall Pine Drive
Sudbury MA 01776
978 443-5000
info@jbpub.com
www.jbpub.com

Jones and Bartlett Publishers Canada
2406 Nikanna Road
Mississauga, ON L5C 2W6
CANADA

Jones and Bartlett Publishers International
Barb House, Barb Mews
London W6 7PA
UK

Copyright © 2004 by Jones and Bartlett Publishers, Inc.

ISBN: 0-7637-4713-0

Printed in the United States of America
07 06 05 04 03   10 9 8 7 6 5 4 3 2 1

Contents

Note-Taking Tips

1. It is easier to take notes if you are not hearing the information for the first time. Read the chapter or the material that is about to be discussed before class. This will help you to anticipate what will be said in class and have an idea of what to write down. It will also help to read over your notes from the previous class. This way you can avoid having to spend the first few minutes of class trying to remember where you left off last time.

2. Don't waste your time trying to write down everything that your professor says. Instead, listen closely and write down only the important points. Review these points after class to remind you of related points that were made during the lecture.

3. If the class discussion takes a spontaneous turn, pay attention and participate in the discussion. Only take notes on the conclusions that are relevant to the lecture.

4. Emphasize main points in your notes. You may want to use a highlighter, special notation (asterisks, exclamation points), format (circle, underline), or placement on the page (indented, bulleted). You will find that when you try to recall these points, you will be able to actually picture them on the page.

5. Be sure to copy specific formulas, laws, and theories word-for-word.

6. Hearing something repeated, stressed, or summed up can be a signal that it is an important concept to understand.

7. Organize handouts, study guides, and exams in your notebook along with your lecture notes. It may be helpful to use a three-ring binder, so that you can insert pages wherever you need to.

8. When taking notes, you might find it helpful to leave a wide margin on all four sides of the page. Doing this allows you to note names, dates, definitions, etc. for easy access and studying later. It may also be helpful to make notes of questions you want to ask your professor about or research later, ideas or relationships that you may want to explore more on your own, or concepts that you don't fully understand.

9. It is best to maintain a separate notebook for each class. Labeling and dating your notes can be helpful when you need to look up information from previous lectures.

10. Make your notes legible, and take notes directly in your notebook. Chances are you won't recopy them no matter how noble your intentions. Spend the time you would have spent recopying the notes studying them instead, drawing conclusions and making connections that you didn't have time for in class.

11. Look over your notes after class while the lecture is still fresh in your mind. Fix illegible items and clarify anything you don't understand. Do this again right before the next class.

Chapter 1: Nutrients and Nourishment

Notes

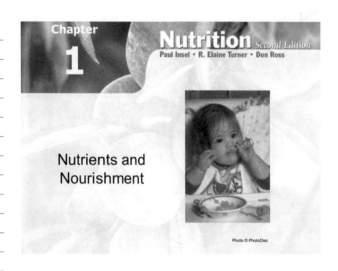

Chapter 1

Nutrition *Second Edition*
Paul Insel • R. Elaine Turner • Don Ross

Nutrients and Nourishment

Photo © PhotoDisc

Influences on Food Choices

- Sensory
  - Taste
    - Sweet, sour, bitter, salty
    - Umami
  - Smell
  - Texture

Influences on Food Choices

- Cognitive
  - Habits
  - Comfort foods
  - Cravings
  - Advertising
  - Social factors
  - Nutritional value
  - Health beliefs

got milk?

Photo courtesy of Bozell Worldwide Inc. as agent for
National Fluid Milk Processor Promotion Board.

Influences on Food Choices

- Culture
  - Beliefs and traditions
  - Religion
  - "American diet"

Photo © PhotoDisc

Introducing the Nutrients

Lipids

Vitamins

Water

Carbohydrates

Minerals

Proteins

- Definition of nutrients
  - Food = mixture of chemicals
  - Nutrients = essential chemicals
  - 6 classes of nutrients

Introducing the Nutrients

- General functions of nutrients
  - Supply energy
    - Carbohydrates, lipids, proteins
  - Contribute to cell and body structure
  - Regulate body processes

Notes

Introducing the Nutrients

- Carbohydrates
  - Sugars and starches
  - Functions
    - Energy source
  - Food sources
    - Grains
    - Vegetables
    - Fruits
    - Dairy products

Photo © PhotoDisc

Introducing the Nutrients

- Lipids
  - Triglycerides (fats and oils), cholesterol and phospholipids
  - Functions
    - Energy source, structure, regulation
  - Food sources
    - Fats and oils
    - Meats
    - Dairy products

Photo © PhotoDisc

Introducing the Nutrients

- Proteins
  - Made of amino acids
  - Functions
    - Energy source, structure, regulation
  - Food sources
    - Meats
    - Dairy products
    - Legumes, vegetables, grains

Photo © PhotoDisc

Introducing the Nutrients

- Vitamins
  - Fat-soluble: A, D, E, K
  - Water-soluble: B vitamins, vitamin C
  - Functions
    - Regulation
  - Food sources
    - All food groups

Photo © PhotoDisc

Introducing the Nutrients

- Minerals
  - Macrominerals and trace minerals
  - Functions
    - Structure, regulation
  - Food sources
    - All food groups

Photo © PhotoDisc

Introducing the Nutrients

- Water
  - Most important nutrient
  - Functions
    - Structure, regulation
  - Food sources
    - Beverages
    - Foods

Photo © PhotoDisc

Notes

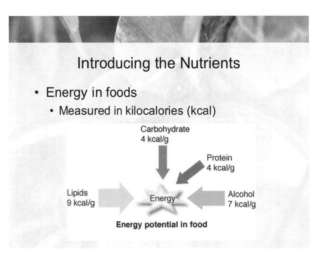

Introducing the Nutrients

- Energy in foods
  - Measured in kilocalories (kcal)

Carbohydrate
4 kcal/g

Protein
4 kcal/g

Lipids
9 kcal/g

Energy

Alcohol
7 kcal/g

Energy potential in food

Applying the Scientific Process to Nutrition

- Scientific method
- Types of studies
  - Epidemiological
  - Animal
  - Cell culture
  - Human
    - Case control
    - Clinical trial

Notes

Chapter 2

Nutrition Second Edition
Paul Insel • R. Elaine Turner • Don Ross

Nutrition
Guidelines
and
Assessment

Linking Nutrients, Foods, and Health

- Choosing a healthful diet
  - Moderation
  - Variety
  - Balance

Dietary Guidelines

- Dietary Guidelines for Americans
  - Aim for Fitness
    - Aim for a healthy weight
    - Be physically active each day
  - Build a Healthy Base
    - Let the Pyramid guide your food choices
    - Choose a variety of grains daily
    - Choose a variety of fruits and vegetables daily
    - Keep food safe to eat

Aim
for Fitness

BUILD
a Healthy Base

CHOOSE
Sensibly

...for good health

Logo courtesy of U.S. Departments of Health and Human Services and Agriculture, http://www.health.gov/dietaryguidelines.

Dietary Guidelines

- Dietary Guidelines for Americans
  - Choose Sensibly
    - Choose a diet that is low in saturated fat and cholesterol, and moderate in total fat
    - Choose beverages and foods to moderate your intake of sugars
    - Choose and prepare foods with less salt
    - If you drink alcoholic beverages, do so in moderation

Food Guide Pyramid

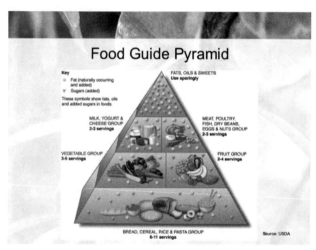

Exchange Lists

- Meal planning for people with diabetes
- Foods grouped by macronutrient content
  - Starches
  - Fruits
  - Milks
  - Other carbohydrates
  - Vegetables
  - Meats and meat substitutes
  - Fats

Notes

Recommendations for Nutrient Intake

- Dietary Reference Intakes (DRIs)
  - Recommendations for nutrient intake
  - Developed by the Food and Nutrition Board
  - Apply to healthy people in the U.S. and Canada
  - Four basic elements

Dietary Reference Intakes (DRIs)

- Estimated Average Requirement (EAR)
  - Amount that meets the nutrient requirements of 50% of people in a life stage/gender group
  - Based on functional indicator of optimal health
- Recommended Dietary Allowance (RDA)
  - Amount that meets the needs of most people in a life stage/gender group

Dietary Reference Intakes (DRIs)

- Adequate Intake (AI)
  - Amount thought to be adequate for most people
  - AI used when EAR and RDA can't be determined

- Tolerable Upper Intake Level (UL)
  - Intake above the UL can be harmful

Dietary Reference Intakes (DRIs)

- Using the DRIs
  - Population groups
    - Assess adequacy of intake
    - Plan diets
    - Set policy and guidelines
  - Individuals
    - Use RDA and AI as target levels for intake
    - Avoid intake > UL

Food Labels

- Mandatory information on food labels
  - Statement of identity
  - Net contents of the package
  - Name and address of manufacturer, packer, distributor
  - List of ingredients
    - Listed in descending order by weight
  - Nutrition information

Food Labels

- Daily Values
  - Compare amount in one serving to the amount recommended for daily consumption

Nutrition Facts

Serving Size: 1 slice (34g/1.2 oz)
Servings Per Container: 20

Amount Per Serving

Calories 90 Calories from fat 10

	% Daily Value*
Total Fat 1g	2%
Saturated Fat 0g	0%
Trans Fat 0g	
Cholesterol 0mg	0%
Sodium 160mg	7%
Total Carbohydrate 15g	2%
Dietary Fiber 2g	8%
Sugars 2g	
Protein 4g	
Vitamin A 0%	Vitamin C 0%
Calcium 0%	Iron 4%

Food Labels: Claims

- Nutrient content claims
  - Descriptive terms, e.g., low fat, high fiber
- Health claims
  - Link one or more dietary components to reduced risk of disease
  - Must be supported by scientific evidence
- Structure/Function claims
  - Describe potential effects on body structure or function

Nutrition Assessment Methods

- Anthropometric Measurements
- Biochemical Tests
- Clinical Observations
- Dietary Intake

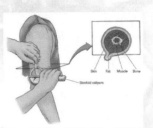

Notes

Nutrition *Second Edition*
Paul Insel • R. Elaine Turner • Don Ross

Spotlight on Complementary and Alternative Nutrition

Photo © PhotoDisc

Functional Foods

- Provide health benefits beyond nutrition
- Phytochemicals
  - Antioxidants
    - Neutralize free radicals
    - Reduce heart disease, cancer risk
  - Found in fruits, vegetables, whole grains, legumes, wine

Food Additives

- Purpose of additives
  - Maintain product consistency
  - Improve nutritional value
  - Maintain quality
  - Provide leavening
  - Enhance flavor or color
- Regulated by FDA
- Subject to Delaney clause

Photos © Corbis Digital Images

Notes

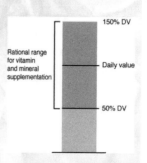

Dietary Supplements: Vitamins and Minerals

- Moderate supplementation
  - Increased nutrient needs and/or poor intake
    - Pregnant and breastfeeding women
    - Women with heavy menstrual losses
    - Children
    - Infants
    - People with severe food restrictions
    - Strict vegetarians
    - Elders
- No more than 150% of DV

150% DV

Rational range for vitamin and mineral supplementation

Daily value

50% DV

Dietary Supplements: Vitamins & Minerals

- Megadoses
  - Conventional medicine
    - Drug interactions
    - Malabsorption syndromes
    - Treatment of deficiencies
    - Drug-like effects
  - Orthomolecular nutrition
    - Proposed for disease prevention
  - Risks: toxicity from large doses

Dietary Supplements: Natural Health Products

- Herbal therapy (phytotherapy)
  - Traditional medical practices
  - Little scientific evidence of efficacy, safety
- Helpful herbs: examples
  - St. John's wort
  - Milk thistle
  - Ginkgo biloba
  - Saw palmetto
  - Cranberry

Photo © PhotoDisc

Dietary Supplements: Natural Health Products

- Harmful herbs
  - Potential for drug interactions
  - Examples of products with toxic side effects
    - Yohimbe
    - Ephedra
    - Chaparral
    - Comfrey
- Other dietary supplements

Dietary Supplements in the Marketplace

- Regulations
  - Dietary Supplement Health and Education Act
  - FTC: advertising
  - FDA: labeling, content
    - No pre-market approval required
    - Supplement Facts panel
    - Claims

Dietary Supplements in the Marketplace

- Claims allowed
  - Health claims (approved by FDA)
  - Nutrient content claims
  - Structure/function claims
    - Link substance and effect on the body
    - No approval required
    - Must have "disclaimer" statement on label

Dietary Supplements in the Marketplace

- Choosing dietary supplements
  - Enough quantity to be effective?
  - How much research has been done?
  - Is it safe?
  - Who is selling the product?
  - Product quality?

Dietary Supplements in the Marketplace

- Fraudulent products
  - Secret cure – "breakthrough"
  - Pseudomedical jargon – "detoxify"
  - Can cure a wide range of diseases
  - Has no side effects, only benefits
  - Backed by 'scientific research' but none is listed

Complementary and Alternative Medicine

- Complementary
  - Practices used in addition to conventional medicine
- Alternative
  - Practices used in place of conventional medicine

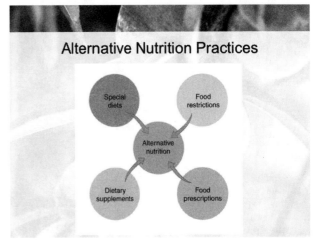

Alternative Nutrition Practices

Nutrition in Complementary and Alternative Medicine

- Vegetarian diets
- Macrobiotic diet
- Food restrictions and prescriptions
- Need for scientific evaluation

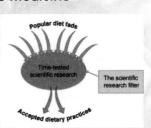

Chapter 3: Digestion and Absorption

Notes

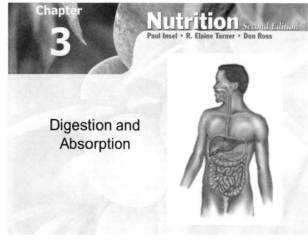

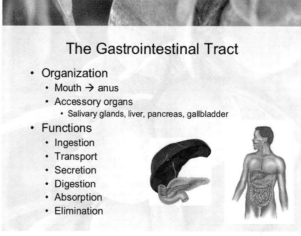

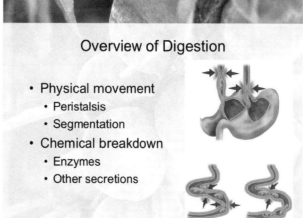

Overview of Absorption

- Absorptive mechanisms
  - Passive diffusion
  - Facilitated diffusion
  - Active transport

Assisting Organs

- Salivary glands
  - Moisten food
  - Supply enzymes
- Liver
  - Produces bile
- Gallbladder
  - Stores and secretes bile
- Pancreas
  - Secretes bicarbonate
  - Secretes enzymes

Putting It All Together: Digestion and Absorption

- Mouth
  - Enzymes
    - Salivary amylase acts on starch
    - Lingual lipase acts on fat
  - Saliva
    - Moistens food for swallowing
- Esophagus
  - Transports food to stomach
  - Esophageal sphincter

Notes

_____
_____
_____
_____
_____
_____
_____
_____
_____
_____
_____
_____
_____
_____
_____
_____
_____
_____
_____
_____
_____
_____
_____
_____
_____
_____
_____
_____
_____
_____
_____
_____
_____
_____
_____
_____
_____
_____

Putting It All Together: Digestion and Absorption

- Stomach
  - Hydrochloric acid
    - Prepares protein for digestion
    - Activates enzymes
  - Pepsin
    - Begins protein digestion
  - Gastric lipase
    - Some fat digestion
  - Gastrin (hormone)
    - Stimulates gastric secretion and movement
  - Intrinsic factor
    - Needed for absorption of vitamin B_{12}

Longitudinal smooth muscle
Circular smooth muscle
Diagonal (oblique) smooth muscle
Pyloric sphincter

Putting It All Together: Digestion and Absorption

- Small intestine
  - Sections of small intestine
    - Duodenum, jejunum, ileum
  - Digestion
    - Bicarbonate neutralizes stomach acid
    - Pancreatic & intestinal enzymes
      - Carbohydrates
      - Fat
      - Protein

Duodenum (10-12 inches)
Most digestion happens here
Jejunum (~4 feet)
Absorbs digested nutrients
Ileum (~5 feet)
Absorbs digested nutrients

Putting It All Together: Digestion and Absorption

- Small intestine
  - Absorption
    - Folds, villi, microvilli expand absorptive surface
    - Most nutrients absorbed here
    - Fat-soluble nutrients go into lymph
    - Other nutrients into blood

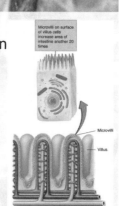

Microvilli on surface of villus cells increase area of intestine another 20 times
Microvilli
Villus

Notes

Putting It All Together: Digestion and Absorption

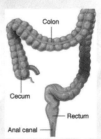

- Large Intestine
  - Digestion
    - Nutrient digestion already complete
    - Some digestion of fiber by bacteria
  - Absorption
    - Water
    - Sodium, potassium, chloride
    - Vitamin K (produced by bacteria)
  - Elimination

Regulation of GI Activity

- Nervous system
  - Regulates GI activity
    - Local system of nerves
    - Central nervous system
- Hormonal system
  - Increases or decreases GI activity

Circulation of Nutrients

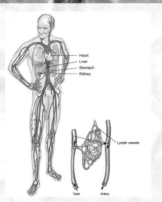

- Vascular system
- Lymphatic system
- Excretion and elimination

Notes

_____

_____

_____

_____

_____

_____

_____

_____

_____

_____

_____

_____

_____

_____

_____

_____

_____

_____

_____

_____

_____

_____

_____

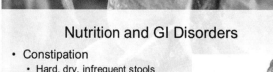

Nutrition and GI Disorders

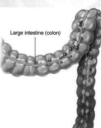

Large intestine (colon)

- Constipation
  - Hard, dry, infrequent stools
  - Reduced by high fiber, fluid intake, exercise
- Diarrhea
  - Loose, watery, frequent stools
  - Symptom of diseases/infections
  - Can cause dehydration
- Diverticulosis
  - Pouches along colon
  - High fiber diet reduces formation

Nutrition and GI Disorders

- Gastroesophageal Reflux Disease (GERD)
  - Reduced by smaller meals, less fat
- Irritable Bowel Syndrome (IBS)
- Colorectal cancer
  - Antioxidants may reduce risk
- Gas
- Ulcers
  - Bacterial cause
- Functional dyspepsia

Chapter 4: Carbohydrates

Notes

Chapter 4

Nutrition *Second Edition*
Paul Insel • R. Elaine Turner • Don Ross

Carbohydrates

Photo © PhotoDisc

Monosaccharides: The Single Sugars

- Monosaccharides – single sugar units
  - Glucose
    - Found in fruits, vegetables, honey
    - "blood sugar" – used for energy
  - Fructose
    - Found in fruits, honey, corn syrup
    - "fruit sugar"
  - Galactose
    - Found as part of lactose in milk

Glucose

Fructose

Galactose

Disaccharides: The Double Sugars

- Disaccharides – two linked sugar units
  - Sucrose: glucose + fructose
    - "table sugar"
    - Made from sugar cane and sugar beets
  - Lactose: glucose + galactose
    - "milk sugar"
    - Found in milk and dairy products
  - Maltose: glucose + glucose
    - Found in germinating cereal grains
    - Product of starch breakdown

Sucrose

Lactose

Maltose

Notes

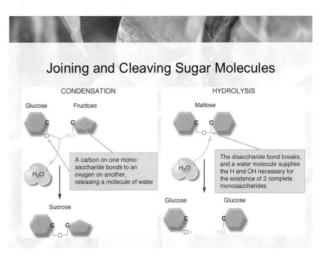

Joining and Cleaving Sugar Molecules

CONDENSATION

Glucose   Fructose

A carbon on one mono-saccharide bonds to an oxygen on another, releasing a molecule of water

H_2O

Sucrose

HYDROLYSIS

Maltose

The disaccharide bond breaks, and a water molecule supplies the H and OH necessary for the existence of 2 complete monosaccharides

H_2O

Glucose   Glucose

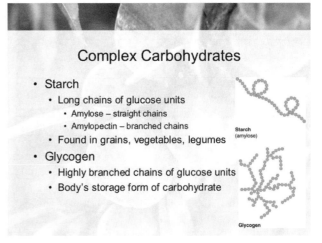

Complex Carbohydrates

- Starch
  - Long chains of glucose units
    - Amylose – straight chains
    - Amylopectin – branched chains
  - Found in grains, vegetables, legumes
- Glycogen
  - Highly branched chains of glucose units
  - Body's storage form of carbohydrate

Starch (amylose)

Glycogen

Complex Carbohydrates: Fiber

- Dietary + Functional = Total Fiber
- Indigestible chains of monosaccharides
  - Non-starch polysaccharides: long chains
    - Cellulose, hemicellulose, pectins, gums, mucilages
    - Lignins
- Found in fruits, vegetables, grains, legumes

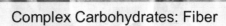

Cellulose fibers

Stachyose

Carbohydrate Digestion and Absorption

- Mouth
  - Salivary amylase begins digestion of starch
- Small intestine
  - Pancreatic amylase completes starch digestion
  - Brush border enzymes digest disaccharides
- End products of carbohydrate digestion
  - Glucose, fructose, galactose
  - Absorbed into bloodstream
- Fibers are not digested, are excreted in feces

Carbohydrates in the Body

- Functions of glucose
  - Energy source
  - Spares body protein
  - Prevents ketosis
  - Excess stored as glycogen
    - In liver and muscle

Glycogen

Carbohydrates in the Body: Regulating Blood Glucose

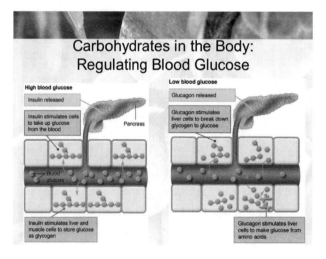

High blood glucose

Insulin released

Insulin stimulates cells to take up glucose from the blood

Pancreas

Blood glucose

Insulin stimulates liver and muscle cells to store glucose as glycogen

Low blood glucose

Glucagon released

Glucagon stimulates liver cells to break down glycogen to glucose

Glucagon stimulates liver cells to make glucose from amino acids

Carbohydrates in the Diet

- Recommended carbohydrate intake
  - AMDR = 45-65% of calories
  - Daily Value (for 2,000 kcal) = 300 grams
  - Dietary Guidelines
    - Variety of grains, fruits, vegetables
    - Moderate sugar intake
  - Current consumption

Carbohydrates in the Diet

- Increasing complex carbohydrate intake
  - Grains, especially whole grains
  - Legumes
  - Vegetables

Carbohydrates in the Diet

- Moderating sugar intake
  - Use less added sugar
  - Limit soft drinks, sugary cereals, candy
  - Choose fresh fruits or those canned in water or juice

Photo © CSquared Studios/PhotoDisc

Notes

_____

_____

_____

_____

_____

_____

_____

_____

_____

_____

_____

_____

_____

_____

_____

_____

_____

_____

_____

_____

_____

_____

_____

_____

Carbohydrates in the Diet

- Nutritive Sweeteners
  - Natural v. refined
  - Sugar alcohols
- Artificial Sweeteners
  - Saccharin
  - Aspartame
  - Acesulfame K
  - Sucralose

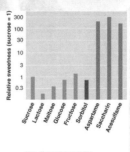

Key   Sugar alcohol ▬
      Refined sweeteners ▨
      Artificial sweetners ▬

Carbohydrates and Health

- High sugar intake
  - Low nutrient content
  - Contributes to tooth decay
  - If excess kcal, contributes to obesity
- High fiber intake
  - Better control of blood glucose
  - Possible reduced cancer risk
  - Reduced risk of heart disease
  - Healthier gastrointestinal functioning

Chapter 5: Lipids

Notes

Lipids

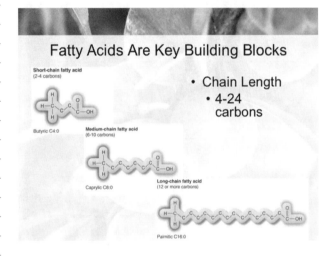

Fatty Acids Are Key Building Blocks

- Chain Length
  - 4-24 carbons

Short-chain fatty acid (2-4 carbons)
Butyric C4:0

Medium-chain fatty acid (6-10 carbons)
Caprylic C8:0

Long-chain fatty acid (12 or more carbons)
Palmitic C16:0

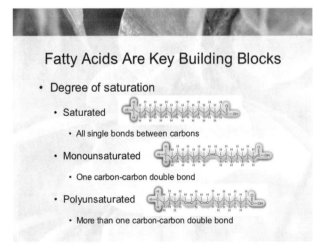

Fatty Acids Are Key Building Blocks

- Degree of saturation
  - Saturated
    - All single bonds between carbons
  - Monounsaturated
    - One carbon-carbon double bond
  - Polyunsaturated
    - More than one carbon-carbon double bond

Notes

Fatty Acids Are Key Building Blocks

- Types of fatty acids
  - *Cis* and *trans*
    - Hydrogenation produces *trans* fatty acids
- Essential fatty acids
  - Linoleic acid and alpha-linolenic acid
  - Can't be made in the body
  - Used to make eicosanoids

Triglycerides

- Structure
  - Glycerol + 3 fatty acids
- Functions
  - Energy source and reserve
  - Insulation and protection
  - Carrier of fat-soluble vitamins
  - Sensory qualities in food

Triglycerides in Food

- Sources of omega-3 fatty acids
  - Soybean, canola, walnut, flaxseed oils
  - Salmon, tuna, mackerel
- Sources of omega-6 fatty acids
  - Vegetable oils
  - Nuts and seeds

Photos © PhotoDisc

Phospholipids

- Structure
  - Glycerol + 2 fatty acids + phosphate group
- Functions
  - Component of cell membranes
  - Lipid transport as part of lipoproteins
  - Emulsifiers
- Food sources
  - Egg yolks, liver, soybeans, peanuts

Sterols: Cholesterol

- Functions
  - Component of cell membranes
  - Precursor to other substances
    - Sterol hormones
    - Vitamin D
    - Bile acids
- Synthesis
  - Made in the liver
- Food sources
  - Found only in animal foods

Digestion and Absorption

- Mouth and stomach
  - Minimal digestion of triglycerides
- Small intestine
  - Emulsified by phospholipids
  - Digested by pancreatic lipase
  - Absorbed into intestinal cells
    - Formed into chylomicrons and moved into lymphatic system

Notes

___

Lipids in the Body

- Lipoproteins carry lipids around the body
  - Chylomicrons
    - Delivers dietary lipids from intestines to cells and liver

Phospholipid / Protein
Cholesterol / Triglyceride / **Chylomicron**

Lipids in the Body

- Very-low-density lipoproteins (VLDL)
  - Deliver triglycerides to cells
- Low-density lipoproteins (LDL)
  - Deliver cholesterol to cells
- High-density lipoproteins (HDL)
  - Pick up cholesterol for removal or recycling

Lipids in the Diet

- Recommended intake
  - Reduce saturated and *trans* fat intake
  - Total fat: 20-35% of calories
  - Need ~ 2% of calories as essential fatty acids
  - Improve balance of omega-3: omega-6 fatty acids

Photos © PhotoDisc

Notes

_____

_____

_____

_____

_____

_____

_____

_____

_____

_____

_____

_____

_____

_____

_____

_____

_____

_____

_____

_____

_____

_____

_____

Lipids in the Diet

- Fat substitutes
  - Different types of composition
  - Olestra
    - Sucrose + fatty acids
    - Indigestible – provides zero kcals
    - Reduces absorption of fat-soluble vitamins

Lipids and Health

- Obesity
  - High fat diets promote weight gain
- Heart disease
  - High saturated and *trans* fat intake raises LDL cholesterol
- Cancer

Chapter 6: Proteins and Amino Acids

Notes

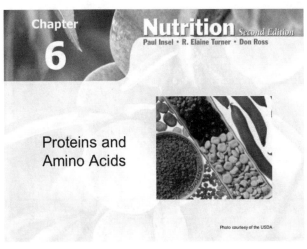

Chapter 6

Nutrition *Second Edition*
Paul Insel • R. Elaine Turner • Don Ross

Proteins and
Amino Acids

Photo courtesy of the USDA

Amino Acids Are the Building Blocks of Protein

- Proteins are sequences of amino acids
- Types of amino acids
  - Essential: most come from diet
  - Nonessential: can be made in the body

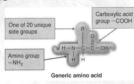

One of 20 unique side groups

Carboxylic acid group —COOH

Amino group —NH₂

Generic amino acid

Amino Acids Are the Building Blocks of Protein

- Protein structure
  - Chain of amino acids
    - Sequence of amino acids determines shape
    - Shape of protein determines function
  - Denaturing protein structure
    - Disrupts function
    - Caused by heat, acid, oxidation, agitation

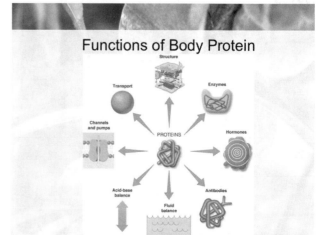

Functions of Body Protein

Protein Digestion and Absorption

- Stomach
  - Proteins are denatured by hydrochloric acid
  - Pepsin begins digestion
- Small intestine
  - Pancreatic and intestinal proteases and peptidases complete digestion
  - Amino acids absorbed into the bloodstream

Proteins in the Body

- Protein synthesis
  - Directed by cellular DNA
- Amino acid pool
- Protein turnover
- Synthesis of non-protein substances

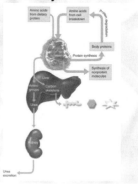

Proteins in the Body

- Protein excretion
  - Deamination of amino acids
  - Amino groups converted to urea for excretion
- Nitrogen balance
  - Nitrogen intake vs. nitrogen output

Proteins in the Diet

- Recommended protein intake
  - Adult RDA = 0.8 grams/kilogram body weight
  - Infant RDA = ~ 1.5 grams/kilogram body weight
- Protein Consumption

Proteins in the Diet

- Protein quality
  - Complete proteins
    - supply all essential amino acids
    - animal proteins, soy proteins
  - Incomplete proteins
    - low in one or more essential amino acids
    - most plant proteins
  - Complementary proteins
    - 2 incomplete proteins = complete protein

Photo © PhotoDisc

Proteins in the Diet

- Evaluating protein quality
  - Amino acid composition
  - Digestibility
  - Protein Digestibility-Corrected Amino Acid
    Score (PDCAAS)
    - Used to determine %DV
- Protein and amino acid supplements
  - Generally not needed with risks unknown

Photo © Jones and Bartlett Publishers

Pros and Cons of Vegetarian Eating

- Types of vegetarian diets
  - Semi-vegetarian
  - Lacto-ovo vegetarian
  - Vegan
- Health benefits vs. health risks
  - Less fat, saturated fat, and cholesterol
  - Restrictive diets may lack nutrients
  - Careful planning needed for children, pregnant women

The Health Effects of Too Little Protein

- Protein-Energy malnutrition (PEM)
  - Kwashiorkor
  - Marasmus

Notes

_____
_____
_____
_____
_____
_____
_____
_____
_____
_____
_____
_____

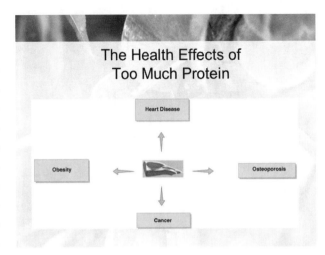

The Health Effects of
Too Much Protein

Heart Disease

Obesity

Osteoporosis

Cancer

Chapter 7: Metabolism

Notes

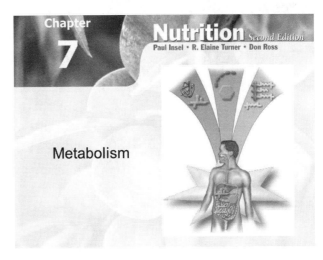

Metabolism

Energy: Fuel for Work

- Energy source
  - Chemical energy in carbohydrates, fat, protein
- Food energy to cellular energy
  - Stage 1: digestion, absorption, transport
  - Stage 2: breakdown of molecules
  - Stage 3: transfer of energy to a form cells can use

What Is Metabolism?

- Catabolism
  - Reactions that breakdown compounds into small units

- Anabolism
  - Reactions that build complex molecules from smaller ones

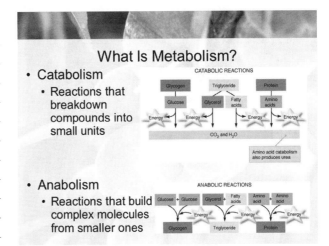

Notes

_____
_____
_____
_____
_____
_____
_____
_____
_____
_____
_____
_____
_____
_____
_____
_____
_____
_____
_____
_____
_____
_____
_____
_____
_____
_____
_____
_____
_____
_____
_____
_____
_____
_____
_____
_____
_____
_____
_____

What Is Metabolism?

- Cell is the metabolic processing center
  - Nucleus
  - Cytoplasm
    - Cytosol + organelles
- ATP is the body's energy currency
  - ATP = adenosine triphosphate
  - Form of energy cells use
- NAD and FAD: transport shuttles
  - Accept high energy electrons for use in ATP production

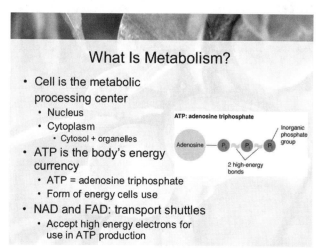

Breakdown and Release of Energy

- Extracting energy from carbohydrate
  - Glycolysis
    - Pathway splits glucose into 2 pyruvates
    - Transfers electrons to NAD
    - Produces some ATP
  - Pyruvate to acetyl CoA
    - Releases CO_2
    - Transfers electrons to NAD

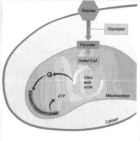

Breakdown and Release of Energy

- Extracting energy from carbohydrate
  - Citric acid cycle
    - Releases CO_2
    - Produces GTP (like ATP)
    - Transfers electrons to NAD and FAD
  - Electron transport chain
    - Accepts electrons from NAD and FAD
    - Produces large amounts of ATP
    - Produces water
  - End products of glucose breakdown
    - ATP, H_2O, CO_2

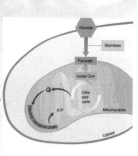

Breakdown and Release of Energy

- Extracting energy from fat
  - Split triglycerides into glycerol and fatty acids
  - Beta-oxidation
    - Breaks apart fatty acids into acetyl CoA
    - Transfers electrons to NAD and FAD
  - Citric acid cycle
    - Acetyl CoA from beta-oxidation enters cycle
  - Electron transport chain
  - End products of fat breakdown
    - ATP, H_2O, CO_2

Breakdown and Release of Energy

- Extracting energy from protein
  - Split protein into amino acids
  - Split off amino group
    - Converted to urea for excretion
  - Carbon skeleton enters breakdown pathways
  - End products
    - ATP, H_2O, CO_2, urea

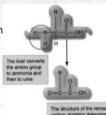

The liver converts the amino group to ammonia and then to urea

The structure of the remaining carbon skeleton determines where it can enter the energy-producing pathways

Breakdown and Release of Energy

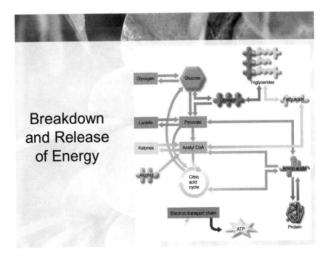

Biosynthesis and Storage

- Making carbohydrate (glucose)
  - Gluconeogenesis
    - Uses pyruvate, lactate, glycerol, certain amino acids
- Storing carbohydrate (glycogen)
  - Liver, muscle make glycogen from glucose
- Making fat (fatty acids)
  - Lipogenesis
    - Uses acetyl CoA from fat, amino acids, glucose
- Storing fat (triglyceride)
  - Stored in adipose tissue

Biosynthesis and Storage

- Making ketone bodies (ketogenesis)
  - Made from acetyl CoA
    - Inadequate glucose in cells
- Making protein (amino acids)
  - Amino acid pool supplied from
    - Diet, protein breakdown, cell synthesis

Regulation of Metabolism

- May favor either anabolic or catabolic functions
- Regulating hormones
  - Insulin
  - Glucagon
  - Cortisol
  - Epinephrine

Notes

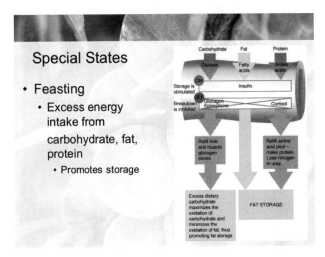

Special States

- Feasting
  - Excess energy intake from carbohydrate, fat, protein
    - Promotes storage

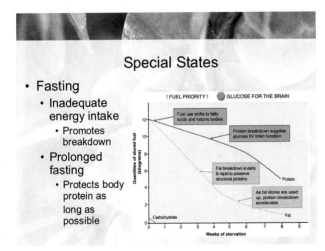

Special States

- Fasting
  - Inadequate energy intake
    - Promotes breakdown
  - Prolonged fasting
    - Protects body protein as long as possible

Notes

Alcohol

- The character of alcohol
  - Ethanol
    - The alcohol in beer, wine, spirits
  - Methanol
    - Wood alcohol – poisonous
- Is alcohol a nutrient?
  - Provides energy
    - 7 kcal/gram
  - No other nutritive value

Photos © PhotoDisc

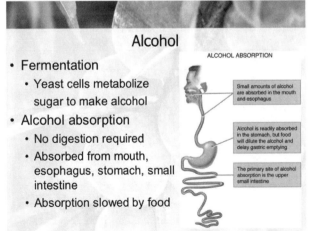

Alcohol

- Fermentation
  - Yeast cells metabolize sugar to make alcohol
- Alcohol absorption
  - No digestion required
  - Absorbed from mouth, esophagus, stomach, small intestine
  - Absorption slowed by food

ALCOHOL ABSORPTION

Small amounts of alcohol are absorbed in the mouth and esophagus

Alcohol is readily absorbed in the stomach, but food will dilute the alcohol and delay gastric emptying

The primary site of alcohol absorption is the upper small intestine

Notes

What is a drink?

Alcohol Metabolism

- Small amount of alcohol
  - Alcohol dehydrogenase
    - Alcohol → acetaldehyde
  - Aldehyde dehydrogenase
    - Acetaldehyde → acetate
  - Metabolites → acetyl CoA → fat

Alcohol Metabolism

- Large amount of alcohol
  - Overwhelms alcohol dehydrogenase system
  - Uses microsomal ethanol-oxidizing system (MEOS)

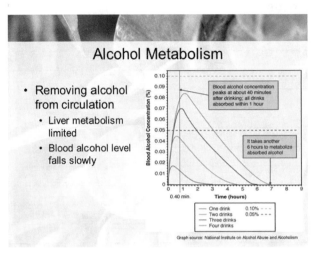

Alcohol Metabolism

- Removing alcohol from circulation
  - Liver metabolism limited
  - Blood alcohol level falls slowly

Alcohol Metabolism: Gender Differences

Body composition
Women have a higher percentage of fat than men (size for size women have less water than men to dilute alcohol).

Less enzyme activity
Alcohol dehydrogenase, the primary enzyme involved in the metabolism of alcohol, is up to 40% less active in women than in men.

Body size
Women are smaller on average than men (smaller livers and less total water).

Hormonal fluctuations
Women typically have a heightened response to alcohol which is increased when they are about to have their periods, or when taking birth control pills.

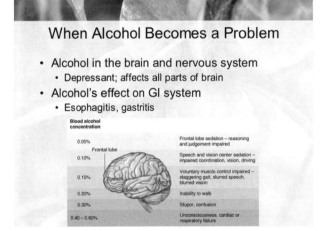

When Alcohol Becomes a Problem

- Alcohol in the brain and nervous system
  - Depressant; affects all parts of brain
- Alcohol's effect on GI system
  - Esophagitis, gastritis

When Alcohol Becomes a Problem

- Alcohol and the liver
  - Fatty liver
  - Fibrosis
  - Cirrhosis
- Fetal alcohol syndrome

Alcoholics and Malnutrition

- Poor diet
  - Alcohol – energy but no nutrients
  - Economic factors
  - Lack of interest in food; GI problems
- Vitamin deficiencies
  - Alcohol interferes with vitamin metabolism
  - Folate, thiamin, vitamin A

Alcoholics and Malnutrition

- Mineral deficiencies
  - Inadequate diet and fluid losses
  - Calcium, magnesium, iron, zinc
  - Some mineral levels are elevated
- Macronutrients
  - Alcohol interferes with amino acid absorption
  - Alcohol raises blood levels of fats
- Body weight

Does Alcohol Have Benefits?

- Moderate drinking associated with reduced mortality
- Heart disease
  - French paradox: red wine

Chapter 8: Energy Balance, Body Composition, and Weight Management

Notes

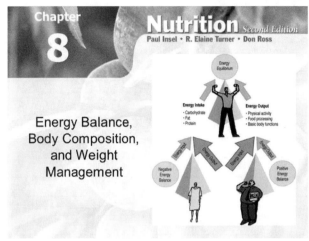

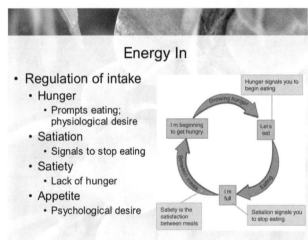

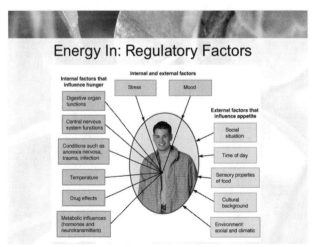

Energy Out: Fuel Uses

- Major components of energy expenditure
  - Resting energy expenditure (REE)
    - Energy for basic body functions
    - Affected by body size, composition, age, gender
  - Physical activity
    - Highly variable
    - Affected by body size, fitness level, type of activity
  - Thermic effect of food (TEF)
    - Energy to digest, absorb, metabolize food

Thermic effect of food (~10%)

Physical activity (15–30%)

Resting energy expenditure (60–75%)

Energy Balance

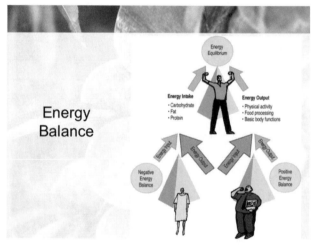

Measuring Energy Expenditure

- Brief history
- Direct vs. indirect calorimetry
- Doubly labeled water

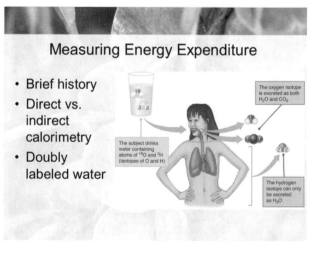

Estimating Energy Expenditure

- EER: Estimated Energy Requirement
  - Predicts total energy expenditure (TEE)
  - Equations for males and females
    - Factors for age, weight, height, physical activity

Body Composition: Understanding Fatness and Weight

- Assessing body weight
  - Height-weight tables
  - Body mass index (BMI)
    - Weight (kg) ÷ height^2 (m)
- Assessing body fatness
- Body fat distribution
  - Waist circumference

When Energy Balance Goes Awry

Healthy weight
Overweight
Obese

Directions: Find your weight on the bottom of the graph. Go straight up from that point until you come to the line that matches your height. Then look to find your weight group.

Height* 6'6"
6'5"
6'4"
6'3"
6'2"
6'1"
6'0"
5'11"
5'10"
5'9"
5'8"
5'7"
5'6"
5'5"
5'4"
5'3"
5'2"
5'1"
5'0"
4'11"
4'10"

50   75   100   125   150   175   200   225   250   275   **Pounds**
23   34   45   57   68   80   91   103   113   125   **Kilograms**

Weight†   *Without shoes. †Without clothes.

- What are the health risks associated with being overweight?

When Energy Balance Goes Awry

- Early theories of weight regulation
  - Fat cell theory
  - Set point theory
- Influences on weight gain and obesity
  - Heredity and genetic factors
  - Sociocultural influences
  - Age and lifestyle factors
  - Gender and ethnicity
  - Socioeconomic factors
  - Psychological factors

Weight Management

- Perception of weight
- Setting realistic goals
- Weight management lifestyle
  - Diet and eating habits
    - Reduce total calories
    - Reduce fat calories
    - Increase complex carbohydrates
    - Improve eating habits
  - Increase physical activity
  - Stress management
  - Self-acceptance

Weight Management

- Weight management approaches
  - Self-help books and manuals
    - Watch for signs of a fad diet
  - Self-help groups
  - Commercial programs
  - Professional counselors
  - Prescription drugs
  - OTC drugs and dietary supplements

Weight Management

- Weight management approaches
  - Surgery

Vertical-banded gastroplasty
Surgery reduces stomach capacity by creating a small pouch

Gastric bypass
Small remaining part of stomach deposits food directly into jejunum

Key
- Gastric bypass
- Vertical-banded gastroplasty

Underweight

- Definition
  - BMI < 18.5 kg/m^2
- Causes
  - Illness
  - Eating disorders
  - Metabolic factors
- Weight-gain strategies
  - Small, frequent meals
  - Fluids between meals
  - High-calorie foods and beverages

Chapter 9: Fat-Soluble Vitamins

Notes

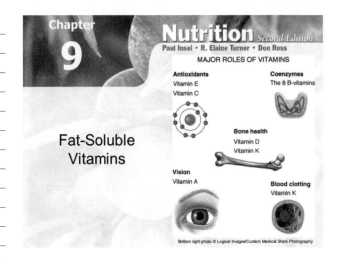

Understanding Vitamins

- A few myths…
  - If a little is good, then a lot is better.
  - Vitamins are energy boosters.
  - Vitamins work exclusively of one another.
- Vitamins in Foods
  - Natural sources: all food groups
  - Enriched and fortified foods

Understanding Vitamins

- Fat-Soluble
  - Vitamins A, D, E, K
  - Absorbed like fat, into lymphatic system
  - Stored in larger quantities, therefore, toxicities may occur
  - May have precursors
  - Less vulnerable to cooking losses

Understanding Vitamins

- Water-Soluble
  - 8 B-vitamins and vitamin C
  - Absorbed into bloodstream
  - Stored in small amounts
  - Vulnerable to cooking losses

Vitamin Absorption

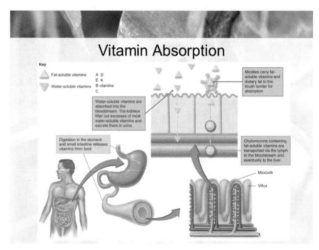

Vitamin A

- Functions
  - Vision, cell development and health, immunity
- Food sources
  - Preformed vitamin A: liver, milk, egg yolks
  - Beta-carotene: yellow/orange fruits and vegetables

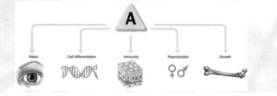

Notes

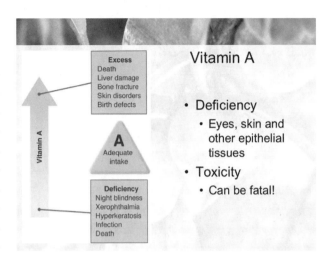

Vitamin A

Excess
Death
Liver damage
Bone fracture
Skin disorders
Birth defects

Vitamin A

A
Adequate
intake

Deficiency
Night blindness
Xerophthalmia
Hyperkeratosis
Infection
Death

- Deficiency
  - Eyes, skin and other epithelial tissues
- Toxicity
  - Can be fatal!

Carotenoids

- Functions
  - Source of vitamin A
  - Antioxidants
  - Other health benefits
- Food Sources
  - Yellow-orange vegetables
  - Orange fruits
  - Dark-green leafy vegetables

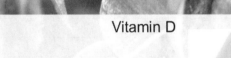

Photo © PhotoDisc

Vitamin D

- Synthesis
  - Made in the skin from cholesterol
  - Activated in liver and kidney
- Functions
  - Regulates blood calcium levels
- Food sources
  - Fortified milk, fortified cereals

Notes

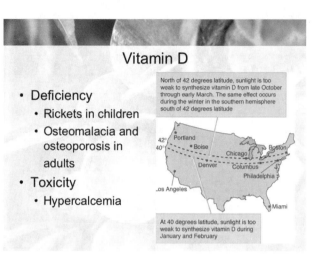

Vitamin D

- Deficiency
  - Rickets in children
  - Osteomalacia and osteoporosis in adults
- Toxicity
  - Hypercalcemia

North of 42 degrees latitude, sunlight is too weak to synthesize vitamin D from late October through early March. The same effect occurs during the winter in the southern hemisphere south of 42 degrees latitude

At 40 degrees latitude, sunlight is too weak to synthesize vitamin D during January and February

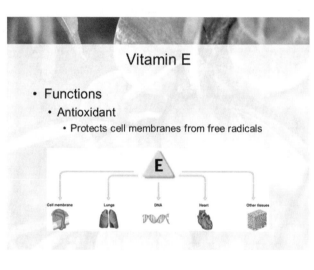

Vitamin E

- Functions
  - Antioxidant
    - Protects cell membranes from free radicals

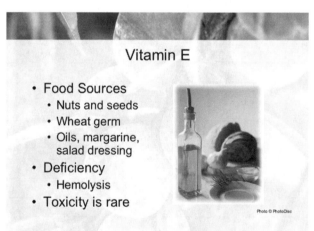

Vitamin E

- Food Sources
  - Nuts and seeds
  - Wheat germ
  - Oils, margarine, salad dressing
- Deficiency
  - Hemolysis
- Toxicity is rare

Photo © PhotoDisc

Notes

_____

_____

_____

_____

_____

_____

_____

_____

_____

_____

_____

_____

_____

_____

_____

_____

_____

_____

_____

_____

_____

_____

_____

_____

Vitamin K

- Functions
  - Blood clotting
  - Formation of bone
- Food sources
  - Green vegetables, liver, egg yolks

Vitamin K

- Deficiency
  - Rare in healthy people
  - Increases risk of hemorrhage
- Excess
  - Can interfere with anticoagulant medications
  - Toxicity is rare

Notes

Water-Soluble Vitamins

Photo © PhotoDisc

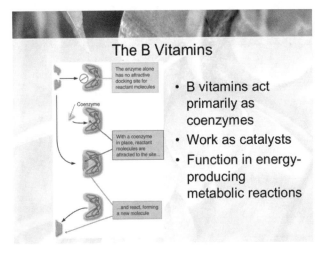

The B Vitamins

The enzyme alone has no attractive docking site for reactant molecules

Coenzyme

With a coenzyme in place, reactant molecules are attracted to the site...

...and react, forming a new molecule

- B vitamins act primarily as coenzymes
- Work as catalysts
- Function in energy-producing metabolic reactions

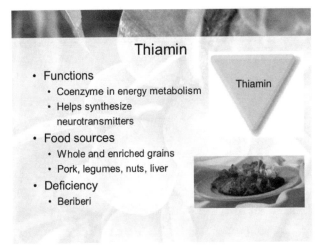

Thiamin

- Functions
  - Coenzyme in energy metabolism
  - Helps synthesize neurotransmitters
- Food sources
  - Whole and enriched grains
  - Pork, legumes, nuts, liver
- Deficiency
  - Beriberi

Thiamin

Notes

Riboflavin

- Functions
  - Coenzyme in energy metabolism
  - Supports antioxidants
- Food sources
  - Milk and dairy products
  - Whole and enriched grains
- Deficiency
  - Ariboflavinosis

Riboflavin

Niacin

- Functions
  - Coenzyme in energy metabolism
  - Supports fatty acid synthesis
- Food sources
  - Whole and enriched grains
  - Meat, poultry, fish, nuts, and peanuts
- Deficiency
  - Pellagra
- Toxicity
  - High doses used to treat high blood cholesterol
  - Side effects: skin flushing, liver damage

Niacin

Pantothenic Acid

- Functions
  - Component of Coenzyme A
- Food sources
  - Widespread in foods
- Deficiency and toxicity are rare.

Pantothenic acid

Notes

_____

_____

_____

_____

_____

_____

_____

_____

_____

_____

_____

_____

_____

_____

_____

_____

_____

_____

_____

_____

_____

_____

_____

_____

_____

_____

_____

_____

_____

_____

_____

_____

_____

_____

_____

_____

_____

Biotin

- Functions
  - Amino acid metabolism
  - Fatty acid synthesis
  - DNA synthesis
- Food sources
  - Cauliflower, liver, peanuts, cheese
- Deficiency and toxicity are rare.

Vitamin B_6

- Functions
  - Coenzyme in protein and amino acid metabolism
  - Supports immune system
- Food sources
  - Meat, fish, poultry, liver
  - Potatoes, bananas, sunflower seeds
- Deficiency
  - Microcytic hypochromic anemia
- Toxicity
  - Can cause permanent nerve damage in high doses

Folate

- Functions
  - Coenzyme in DNA synthesis and cell division
  - Needed for normal red blood cell synthesis
- Food sources
  - Green leafy vegetables, orange juice, legumes
  - Fortified cereals, enriched grains

Folate

- Deficiency
  - Megaloblastic anemia
  - Can contribute to neural tube defects
  - Women of childbearing age need 400 micrograms/day of folic acid
- Toxicity
  - Can mask vitamin B_{12} deficiency

SPINE AFFECTED BY SPINA BIFIDA

Skin on back
Spinal fluid
Spinal cord
Vertebra

Vitamin B_{12}

- Functions
  - Needed for normal folate function
    - DNA and red blood cell synthesis
  - Maintains myelin sheath around nerves
- Food sources
  - Only animal foods: meats, liver, milk, eggs
- Deficiency
  - Pernicious anemia
    - Megaloblastic anemia + nerve damage

B_{12}

Vitamin C

- Functions
  - Antioxidant
  - Needed for collagen synthesis
- Food sources
  - Fruits: citrus, strawberries, kiwi
  - Vegetables: broccoli, tomatoes, potatoes
- Deficiency
  - Scurvy
- Toxicity
  - May cause GI distress in high doses

C

Notes

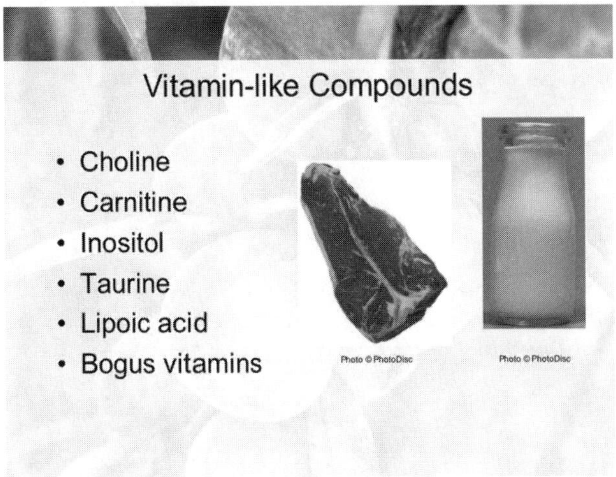

_____

_____

_____

_____

_____

_____

_____

_____

_____

_____

Vitamin-like Compounds

- Choline
- Carnitine
- Inositol
- Taurine
- Lipoic acid
- Bogus vitamins

Photo © PhotoDisc

Photo © PhotoDisc

Chapter 11: Water and Major Minerals

Notes

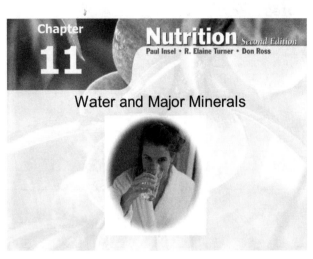

Chapter 11

Nutrition *Second Edition*
Paul Insel • R. Elaine Turner • Don Ross

Water and Major Minerals

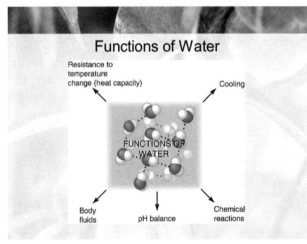

Functions of Water

Resistance to temperature change (heat capacity)

Cooling

FUNCTIONS OF WATER

Body fluids

pH balance

Chemical reactions

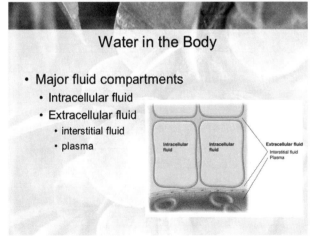

Water in the Body

- Major fluid compartments
  - Intracellular fluid
  - Extracellular fluid
    - interstitial fluid
    - plasma

Intracellular fluid

Intracellular fluid

Extracellular fluid
Interstitial fluid
Plasma

Notes

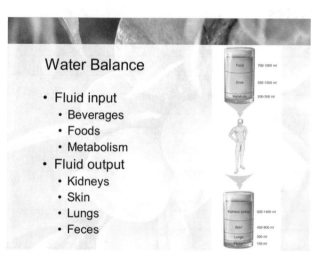

Water Balance

- Fluid input
  - Beverages
  - Foods
  - Metabolism
- Fluid output
  - Kidneys
  - Skin
  - Lungs
  - Feces

Regulation of Water Balance

- Hormonal effects
  - Antidiuretic hormone (ADH)
  - Aldosterone
- Thirst
- Substances that affect water balance
  - Alcohol, caffeine, and diuretic medications

Mineral Bioavailability

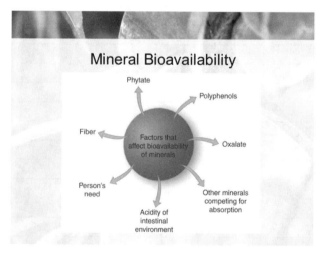

Sodium

- Functions
  - Fluid balance
  - Nerve impulse transmission
- Food sources and recommended intake
  - Salt
  - Processed and convenience foods
  - Limit to 2,400 milligrams/day (DV)

Potassium

- Functions
  - Muscle contraction
  - Nerve impulse transmission
  - Fluid balance
- Food sources
  - Unprocessed foods: fruits, vegetables, grains

Photo © PhotoDisc

Chloride

- Functions of chloride
  - Fluid balance
  - Hydrochloric acid (stomach acid)
- Food sources of chloride
  - Table salt

Notes

Calcium

- Functions
  - Bone structure
  - Blood clotting
  - Nerve impulse transmission, muscle contraction
- Food sources
  - Milk and dairy products
  - Green vegetables, tofu, fortified foods

Calcium

Regulation of Blood Calcium

- Hormones
  - Vitamin D
  - Parathyroid hormone
  - Calcitonin
- Target tissues
  - Small intestine
  - Kidneys
  - Bone

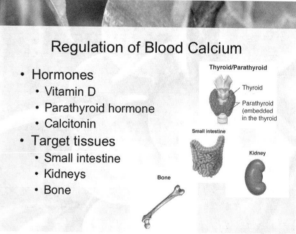

Thyroid/Parathyroid

Thyroid

Parathyroid (embedded in the thyroid)

Small intestine

Kidney

Bone

Phosphorus

- Functions
  - Bone structure
  - Component of ATP, DNA, RNA, phospholipids
- Food sources
  - Meat, milk, eggs
  - Processed foods

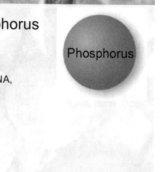

Phosphorus

Magnesium

- Functions
  - DNA and protein synthesis
  - Blood clotting, muscle contraction, ATP production
- Food sources
  - Whole grains, vegetables, legumes, tofu, seafood

Photo © PhotoDisc

Major Minerals and Health

- Hypertension
  - High blood pressure
  - Affects nearly 25% of adult Americans
- Osteoporosis
  - "porous bone"
  - Affects more than 25 million Americans and is the leading cause of bone fractures in older adults

Chapter 12: Trace Minerals

Notes

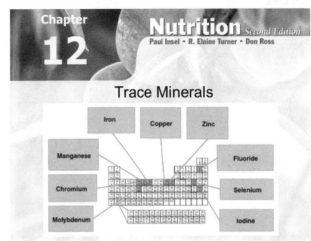

What Are Trace Minerals?

- Needed in small amounts in the diet
  - <100 mg/day
- Found in small amounts in the body
- Crucial to many body functions, including metabolic pathways

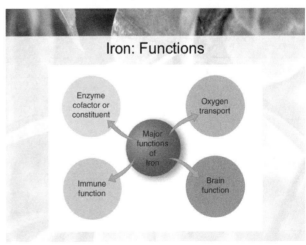

Notes

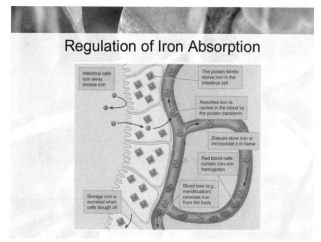

Regulation of Iron Absorption

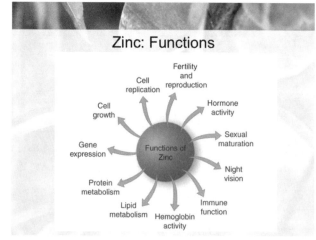

Iron

- Food sources
  - Red meats, liver, seafood
- Deficiency
  - Iron-deficiency anemia
- Toxicity
  - Poisoning in children
  - Hemochromatosis
  - Iron overload

Photo © PhotoDisc

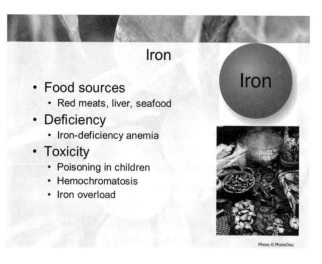

Zinc: Functions

Fertility and reproduction

Cell replication

Hormone activity

Cell growth

Sexual maturation

Gene expression

Functions of Zinc

Night vision

Protein metabolism

Immune function

Lipid metabolism

Hemoglobin activity

Notes

Zinc

- Food sources
  - Red meats, seafood
- Deficiency
  - Poor growth, delayed development
- Toxicity
  - Can cause copper deficiency

Zinc

Selenium

- Functions
  - Part of antioxidant enzyme
  - Thyroid metabolism, immune function
- Food sources
  - Organ meats, seafood, meats
- Deficiency
  - Increases susceptibility to some infections
- Toxicity
  - Brittle hair and nails

Selenium

Photo © PhotoDisc

Iodine

- Functions
  - Thyroid hormone production
- Food sources
  - Iodized salt, fish, seafood, dairy products
- Deficiency
  - Goiter: enlarged thyroid gland
  - Cretinism: mental retardation
    - Occurs in fetus when pregnant woman is deficient

Iodine

Notes

_____

_____

_____

_____

_____

_____

_____

_____

_____

_____

_____

_____

_____

_____

_____

_____

_____

_____

_____

_____

_____

_____

_____

_____

_____

_____

_____

_____

_____

_____

_____

Copper

- Functions
  - Melanin, collagen, elastin production
  - Immune function
  - Antioxidant enzyme systems
- Food sources
  - Organ meats, shellfish, nuts, legumes

Manganese

- Functions
  - Cartilage production
  - Antioxidant enzyme systems
- Food sources
  - Tea, nuts, cereals

Fluoride

- Functions
  - Bone and tooth structure
- Food sources
  - Fluoridated water
- Fluoride balance
  - Excess can cause fluorosis

Notes

_____

_____

_____

_____

_____

_____

_____

_____

_____

_____

_____

Chromium

- Functions
  - Glucose metabolism
- Food sources
  - Mushrooms, dark chocolate, nuts, whole grains

Chapter 13: Sports Nutrition

Notes

Chapter 13

Nutrition *Second Edition*
Paul Insel • R. Elaine Turner • Don Ross

Sports Nutrition

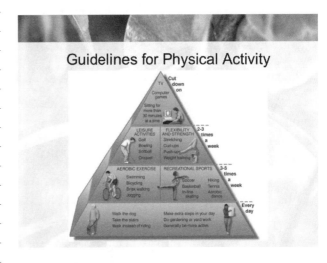

Guidelines for Physical Activity

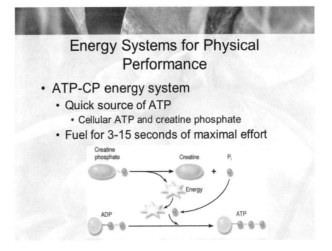

Energy Systems for Physical Performance

- ATP-CP energy system
  - Quick source of ATP
    - Cellular ATP and creatine phosphate
  - Fuel for 3-15 seconds of maximal effort

Notes

_____

_____

_____

_____

_____

_____

_____

_____

_____

_____

_____

_____

_____

_____

_____

_____

_____

_____

_____

_____

_____

_____

_____

_____

_____

_____

_____

_____

_____

_____

_____

_____

_____

_____

_____

_____

_____

_____

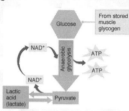

Energy Systems for Physical Performance

- Lactic acid energy system
  - Breakdown of glucose to lactic acid (lactate)
    - Doesn't require oxygen
  - Rise in acidity triggers muscle fatigue

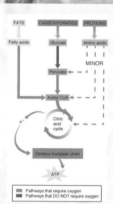

Energy Systems for Physical Performance

- Oxygen energy system
  - Breakdown of carbohydrate and fat for energy
    - Requires oxygen
    - Produces ATP more slowly

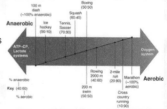

Energy Systems for Physical Performance

- Teamwork in energy production
  - Anaerobic systems for short duration activities, early part of endurance activities
  - Aerobic systems for endurance activities
- Training
  - Decreases reliance on anaerobic systems
  - Extends availability of glycogen

Optimal Nutrition for Athletic Performance

- Consume adequate energy and nutrients
- Maintain appropriate body composition
- Promote optimal recovery from training
- Maintain hydration status

Carbohydrate and Exercise

- High carbohydrate diets
  - Increase glycogen stores
  - Extend endurance
- Carbohydrate loading
- Carbohydrate intake
  - Before exercise
  - During exercise
  - After exercise

Dietary Fat and Exercise

- Major fuel source for endurance activities
- High fat diet not needed
- Recommendations
  - Moderate fat intake

Notes

Protein and Exercise

- Protein recommendations
  - Adults: 0.8 grams/kg body weight
  - Endurance athletes: 1.2-1.4 grams/kg
  - Strength athletes: 1.6-1.7 grams/kg
- Protein sources
  - Foods: lean meats, fish, low-fat dairy, egg whites
- Protein intake after exercise
  - Helps replenish glycogen
- Dangers of high protein intake

Vitamins, Minerals, and Athletic Performance

- B vitamins
  - Needed for energy metabolism
  - Choose variety of whole grains, fruits, vegetables
- Calcium
  - Needed for normal muscle function, strong bones
  - Low-fat dairy products
  - Adequate intake may be a problem for females
- Iron
  - Needed for oxygen delivery and energy production
  - Athletes have higher losses
  - Lean red meats, vegetables, enriched grains

Fluid Needs During Exercise

- Exercise and fluid loss
  - Increased losses from sweat
  - Increased with heat, humidity
  - Risk for dehydration
- Hydration
  - Adequate fluids before, during, after exercise
  - Water vs. sports drinks

Every 15 minutes, cyclists were given drinks either:
- containing carbohydrate
- containing no carbohydrate (flavored water)

Notes

Nutrition Supplements and Ergogenic Aids

- Many product claims
  - Energy, enhance performance, change body composition
- Limited scientific evidence
- Potential for side effects
- Many substances are banned for athletes

Weight and Body Composition

- Weight gain
  - Increase muscle, reduce fat
- Weight loss
  - Lose fat, maintain muscle
  - Avoid dangerous weight loss practices
- Female athlete triad
  - Disordered eating
  - Amenorrhea
  - Osteoporosis

Notes

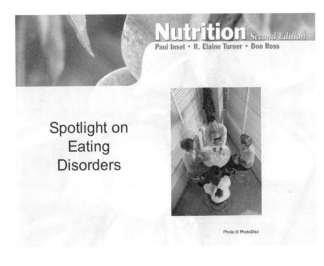

Nutrition *Second Edition*
Paul Insel • R. Elaine Turner • Don Ross

Spotlight on
Eating
Disorders

Photo © PhotoDisc

Eating Disorders

- Eating disorders vs. disordered eating
- The eating disorder continuum

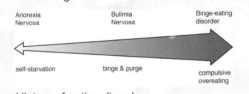

Anorexia Nervosa	Bulimia Nervosa	Binge-eating disorder
self-starvation	binge & purge	compulsive overeating

- History of eating disorders

Eating Disorders: No Simple Causes

- Predisposition
- Social factors
  - Expectations for body size, shape
- Psychological factors
  - Peer relationships, family expectations, emotional trauma
- Biological factors
  - Neurotransmitter levels
- Genetic factors
  - Synthesis and release of leptin, orexin

Notes

Anorexia Nervosa

- Diagnostic criteria
  - Body weight < 85% of expected (BMI ≤ 17.5 kg/m^2)
  - Intense fear of weight gain
  - Distorted body image
  - Amenorrhea
- Causes
- Warning signs

Anorexia Nervosa: Treatment

- Goals
  - Stabilize physical condition
  - Convert patient into participant
- Restoring nutritional status
- Gradual weight gain
- Psychotherapy
  - Individual
  - Group
  - Family

Bulimia Nervosa

- Diagnostic criteria
  - Recurrent binge eating
  - Recurrent purging, excessive exercise, fasting
  - Excessive concern about weight, shape
  - Absence of anorexia nervosa
- Causes

Notes

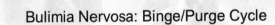

Bulimia Nervosa: Binge/Purge Cycle

- Binge: large amount of food, short period of time
  - High calorie, high fat foods
- Purge
  - Affects fluid and electrolyte balance
  - Can be life-threatening

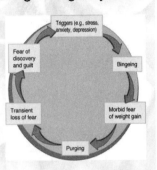

Bulimia Nervosa: Treatment

- Medical
- Nutritional
- Psychotherapy
  - Antidepressant medications

Binge-Eating Disorder

- Diagnostic criteria
  - Recurrent binge eating
  - Distress over eating behaviors
  - No recurrent purging
  - Absence of anorexia nervosa
- Triggers of binge eating
  - Stress
  - Conflict
  - Frequent dieting

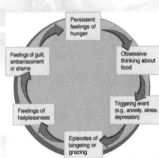

Binge-Eating Disorder: Treatment

- Psychotherapy
  - Antidepressant medications
- Long-term support

Eating Disorders: Related Issues

- Males: an overlooked population
  - Fewer instances than females
  - Men involved in sports, modeling, entertainment
    - Pressure for certain weight, shape
- Anorexia athletica
  - Sports-related eating disorders
  - Body size/shape important in competition
  - Pressure from coaches

Eating Disorders: Related Issues

- Female athlete triad
  - Disordered eating
  - Amenorrhea
  - Osteoporosis

Eating Disorders: Related Issues

- Vegetarianism and eating disorders
- Smoking and eating disorders
- Baryophobia
- Infantile anorexia

Preventing Eating Disorders

- Promote self-esteem
- Size acceptance
- Celebrate the diversity in all sizes and shapes
- Discourage meal skipping
- Encourage eating in response to hunger, not emotions

Notes

Chapter 14

Nutrition *Second Edition*
Paul Insel • R. Elaine Turner • Don Ross

Life Cycle:
Maternal and
Infant
Nutrition

Pregnancy

- Nutrition before conception
  - Risk assessment, health promotion, intervention
  - Weight
    - Maintain a healthy weight
  - Vitamins
    - 400 micrograms folic acid/day
    - Avoid high doses of retinol
  - Substance use
    - Eliminate prior to pregnancy

Photo © PhotoDisc

Pregnancy

- Physiology of pregnancy
  - Stages of human fetal growth
    - Blastogenic stage: first 2 weeks
      - Cells differentiate into fetus, placenta
    - Embryonic stage: weeks 3-8
      - Development of organ systems
    - Fetal stage: week 9-delivery
      - Growth

Notes

Pregnancy
- Physiology of pregnancy
  - Maternal changes
    - Growth of adipose, breast, uterine tissues
    - Increase blood volume
    - Slower GI motility

Blood volume and red blood cell mass increase
Heart rate increases by 20%
Hormones promote growth and changes in breast tissue
Curvature of spine increases
Fat stores increase
Uterus expands
Gastrointestinal motility slows

Pregnancy
- Maternal weight gain
  - Recommendations depend on BMI
    - Normal weight (BMI = 19.8 – 26 kg/m^2)
      - Gain 25-35 pounds
- Energy and nutrition during pregnancy
  - Energy
    - Support adequate weight gain
  - Macronutrients
    - High carbohydrate, moderate fat and protein

Pregnancy
- Energy and nutrition during pregnancy
  - Micronutrients
    - Increase need for most vitamins and minerals
    - Highest increase for iron and folate
- Food choices for pregnant women
  - Pyramid-style diet
  - Supplements of iron and folate
- Substance use
  - Risk for birth defects, low birth weight, preterm delivery

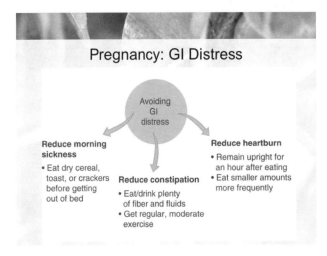

Pregnancy: GI Distress

Avoiding GI distress

Reduce morning sickness
- Eat dry cereal, toast, or crackers before getting out of bed

Reduce constipation
- Eat/drink plenty of fiber and fluids
- Get regular, moderate exercise

Reduce heartburn
- Remain upright for an hour after eating
- Eat smaller amounts more frequently

Lactation

- Physiology of lactation
- Changes during pregnancy
  - Increased breast tissue
  - Maturation of structure
- Hormonal controls
  - Prolactin: stimulates milk production
  - Oxytocin: stimulates milk release
    - "let-down" reflex

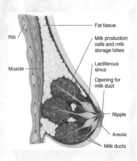

Lactation

- Nutrition for breastfeeding women
  - Energy and protein
    - Higher needs than pregnancy
  - Vitamins and minerals
    - Most are higher or same as pregnancy
    - Iron and folate needs are lower
  - Water
- Food choices
- Practices to avoid while breastfeeding
  - Alcohol, drugs, smoking, excess caffeine

Lactation

- Benefits of breastfeeding
  - Benefits for infants
    - Optimal nutrition
    - Reduced incidence of respiratory, GI, ear infections
    - Convenience
    - Other benefits
  - Benefits for mother
    - Convenience
    - Enhanced recovery of uterus size
    - Other benefits
- Contraindications to breastfeeding

Infancy

- Growth is the best marker of nutritional status
  - Evaluated using growth charts
- Weight gain
  - Double birth weight by 4-6 months
  - Triple birth weight by 12 months
- Length gain
  - Increase length by 50% by 12 months
- Head circumference

Infancy

- Energy and nutrient needs of infants
  - Requirements based on composition of breast milk
  - Energy
    - Highest needs of any life stage
  - Protein
    - Highest needs of any life stage
  - Carbohydrate and fat
    - Fat: major energy source
    - Carbohydrates: simple sugars
  - Water

Protein
Growth

Carbohydrate
(lactose)
Energy
Enhances absorption of calcium and phosphorus

Fat
Energy
Nervous system development
Accumulation of fat stores

Notes

Infancy

- Energy and nutrient needs of infants
  - Key vitamins and minerals
  - Feeding infants
    - Breastfeeding
    - Infant formula

Infancy

- Introduction of solid foods
  - Readiness for solids
    - Increased digestive enzymes
    - Loss of extrusion reflex
    - Able to sit without support
    - Age of about 4-6 months
  - Feeding schedule
    - Baby rice cereal
    - Strained fruits, vegetables, meats
    - Add one food at a time

Notes

Life Cycle:
From Childhood
Through Adulthood

Photo © PhotoDisc

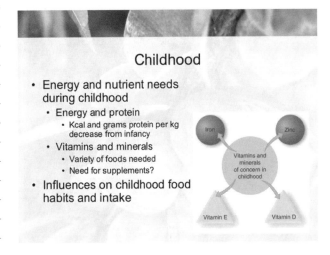

Childhood

- Energy and nutrient needs during childhood
  - Energy and protein
    - Kcal and grams protein per kg decrease from infancy
  - Vitamins and minerals
    - Variety of foods needed
    - Need for supplements?
- Influences on childhood food habits and intake

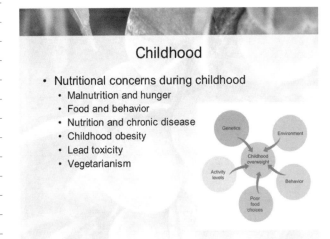

Childhood

- Nutritional concerns during childhood
  - Malnutrition and hunger
  - Food and behavior
  - Nutrition and chronic disease
  - Childhood obesity
  - Lead toxicity
  - Vegetarianism

Adolescence

- Physical growth and development
  - Adolescent growth spurt
    - Boys: begins between 12-13 years
      - Gain about 8 inches in height, 45 pounds in weight
    - Girls: begins between 10-11 years
      - Gain about 6 inches in height, 35 pounds in weight
  - Changes in body composition
  - Changes in emotional maturity

Adolescence

- Nutrient needs of adolescents
  - Energy and protein
    - Highest total calories and protein grams per day
  - Vitamins and minerals

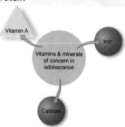

Adolescence

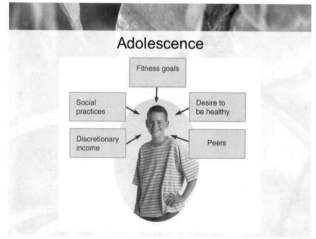

Notes

Adolescence

- Nutrition-related concerns of adolescents
  - Fitness and sports
  - Acne
  - Eating disorders
  - Obesity
  - Tobacco, alcohol, recreational drugs

Staying Young While Growing Older

- Age-related changes
  - Weight and body composition
    - Add fat, lose lean body mass
  - Mobility
    - Reduced muscle and skeletal strength
  - Immunity
    - Decline in defense mechanism
  - Taste and smell
    - Decline in ability
  - Gastrointestinal changes
    - Reduced acid secretion, reduced motility

Photo © PhotoDisc

Nutrient Needs of the Mature Adult

- Energy
  - Reduced needs
    - Decreased activity, decreased lean body mass
- Protein
  - Same needs per kg body weight as younger adults
- Carbohydrate
  - More likely to be lactose intolerant
- Fat
  - Maintain moderate-low fat diet
- Water
  - Reduced thirst response

Notes

Nutrient Needs of the Mature Adult

Nutrition-Related Concerns of Mature Adults

- Drug-drug and drug-nutrient interactions
  - Can affect use of drugs or nutrients
- Depression
  - May reduce food intake
  - Alcoholism can interfere with nutrient use
- Anorexia of aging
  - Loss of appetite with illness
  - Can lead to protein-energy malnutrition

Nutrition-Related Concerns of Mature Adults

- Arthritis
  - May interfere with food preparation and eating
  - Dietary changes may improve symptoms
- Bowel and bladder regulation
  - Increased risk of urinary tract infection
  - Chronic constipation more common with age
    - Need for increased fluids, fiber
- Dental health
  - May interfere with eating ability, food choices

Nutrition-Related Concerns of Mature Adults

- Vision problems
  - Can affect ability to shop, cook
  - Antioxidants may reduce macular degeneration
- Osteoporosis
  - Common in elders, especially women
  - Maintain calcium, vitamin D, exercise
- Alzheimer's disease
  - Affects ability to function
  - Reduced taste, smell
  - Risk for weight loss, malnutrition

Meal Management for Mature Adults

- Managing independently
  - Services for elders
    - Meals on Wheels
    - Elderly Nutrition Program
    - Food Stamp Program
- Wise eating for one or two
- Finding community resources

Notes

_____

Chapter
16

Nutrition *Second Edition*

Paul Insel • R. Elaine Turner • Don Ross

Diet and Health

Photo © PhotoDisc   Photo © PhotoDisc

Nutrition and Chronic Disease

- Healthy People 2010
  - Disease prevention/health promotion objectives
    - Increase the quality and years of healthy life
    - Eliminate health disparities
- Obesity and chronic disease
- Physical inactivity and chronic disease

Genetics and Disease

- Disease risk factors
  - Genetics, environment, nutrition, lifestyle
- Human Genome Project
  - International effort designed to help understand the genetics of diseases
  - Spearheaded by NIH

Notes

Genetics and Disease

- DNA and genes
  - Genetic code for making proteins
  - Mutations: error in genetic code
- Nutritional genomics
  - Influence of diet on gene expression

Cardiovascular Disease (CVD)

- Leading cause of death in U.S. and Canada
- Major type: atherosclerosis

Aortic arch
Left pulmonary artery
Auricle of left atrium
Left coronary artery
Left ventricle
Descending aorta
Ascending aorta
Right atrium
Right coronary artery
Right ventricle

Atherosclerosis

- Definition
  - Role of cholesterol
  - Role of inflammation
- Risk Factors

Atherosclerosis: Reducing the Risk

- Fatty acids and cholesterol
- Omega-3 fatty acids
- Fiber
- B vitamins
- Antioxidants

- Soy
- The French Paradox
- The Mediterranean Diet
- Physical activity

Hypertension

- Definition
- Risk factors

Hypertension: Reducing the Risk

- Sodium
- Other minerals
- DASH diet
  - Rich in fruits and vegetables
  - Low-fat dairy products
  - Low in fat, saturated fat, cholesterol

Notes

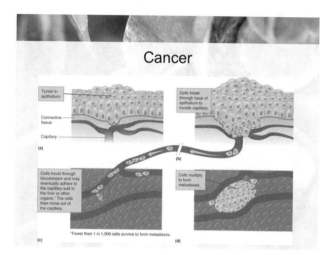

Cancer

- Risk factors
- Reducing the risk
  - Eat a variety of healthful foods
    - emphasis on plant sources
  - Adopt a physically active lifestyle
  - Maintain a healthful weight throughout life
  - If you drink alcoholic beverages, limit consumption

Diabetes

- Definition and types
  - Type 1
  - Type 2
  - Pre-diabetes
  - Gestational
- Risk factors
- Reducing the risk
- Management
  - Diet
  - Physical activity
  - medications

Metabolic Syndrome

- Cluster of three of the following risk factors:
  - Excess abdominal fat
  - High blood glucose
  - High serum triglycerides
  - Low HDL cholesterol
  - Hypertension

Osteoporosis

- Definition
  - "Porous bone"
- Risk factors
- Reducing the risk
  - Calcium and D
  - Weight-bearing exercise

Notes

Nutrition Second Edition
Paul Insel • R. Elaine Turner • Don Ross

Chapter 17

Food Safety

Food Safety

- Harmful substances in foods
  - Pathogens
    - Bacteria, viruses, parasites
    - Foodborne illness
      - Infection from pathogen
      - Toxin produced by microorganism

Food Safety

- Common causes of foodborne illness
  - *Staphylococcus aureus*
  - *Clostridium botulinum*
  - *Salmonella enteriditis*
  - *Escherichia coli*

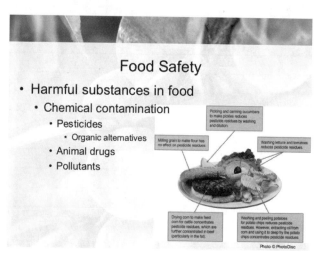

Food Safety

- Harmful substances in food
  - Chemical contamination
    - Pesticides
      - Organic alternatives
    - Animal drugs
    - Pollutants

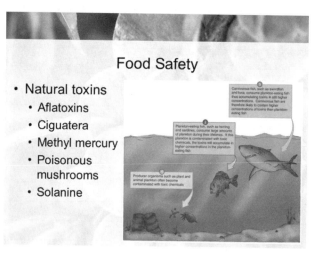

Food Safety

- Natural toxins
  - Aflatoxins
  - Ciguatera
  - Methyl mercury
  - Poisonous mushrooms
  - Solanine

Food Safety: Government's Role

Food Safety: Food Industry's Role

- Hazard Analysis Critical Control Point (HACCP) – 7 steps
  - Analyze hazards
  - Identify critical control points
  - Establish preventive measures with critical limits
  - Establish procedures to monitor control points
  - Establish corrective actions if critical limit isn't met
  - Establish effective record keeping
  - Establish procedures to verify that the system is working consistently

Food Safety: Consumer's Role

- Keeping food safe
  - Clean
  - Separate
  - Cook
  - Chill

FIGHT BAC!
Keep Food Safe From Bacteria ™

CLEAN
Wash hands and surfaces often.

SEPARATE
Don't cross-contaminate.

CHILL
Refrigerate promptly.

COOK
Cook to proper temperatures.

Illustration courtesy of Partnership for Food Safety Education

Risk for Foodborne Illness

- Immune disorders
- Cancer
- Diabetes
- Long-term steroid use
- Liver disease
- Hemochromatosis
- Stomach problems

Notes

Food Technology

- Food preservation
  - Preservatives
    - Salt, sugar
    - Antioxidants
  - Other preservation techniques
    - Salting
    - Fermenting
    - Drying
    - Canning
    - Heating (e.g. pasteurization)
    - Irradiation

Preservatives

Pasteurization

Irradiation

Photos © Corbis Digital Images

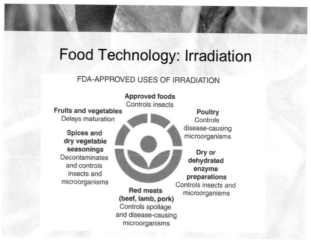

Food Technology: Irradiation

FDA-APPROVED USES OF IRRADIATION

Approved foods
Controls insects

Fruits and vegetables
Delays maturation

Poultry
Controls disease-causing microorganisms

Spices and dry vegetable seasonings
Decontaminates and controls insects and microorganisms

Dry or dehydrated enzyme preparations
Controls insects and microorganisms

Red meats (beef, lamb, pork)
Controls spoilage and disease-causing microorganisms

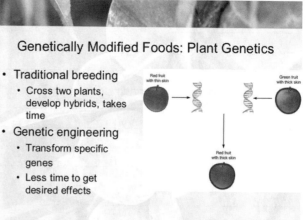

Genetically Modified Foods: Plant Genetics

- Traditional breeding
  - Cross two plants, develop hybrids, takes time
- Genetic engineering
  - Transform specific genes
  - Less time to get desired effects

Red fruit with thin skin

Green fruit with thick skin

Red fruit with thick skin

Notes

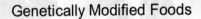

Genetically Modified Foods

- Benefits of genetic engineering
  - Enhanced plant growth
  - Reduced pesticide, fertilizer use
  - Enhanced nutrient composition
  - Enhanced crop yields
- Risks
  - Potential for new allergens
  - Herbicide resistant weeds
  - Loss of biodiversity

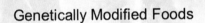

Genetically Modified Foods

- Regulation
  - FDA oversees GM foods
  - Required labeling
    - If food is significantly different
    - If there are issues regarding use of the food
    - If food has different nutritional properties
    - If new food contains unexpected allergen

Chapter 18: World View of Nutrition

Notes

Chapter 18

Nutrition *Second Edition*
Paul Insel • R. Elaine Turner • Don Ross

World View of Nutrition

A few definitions…

- Hunger
  - Uneasy or painful sensation caused by lack of food
- Malnutrition
  - Failure to achieve nutrient requirements
- Food insecurity
  - Limited or uncertain availability of nutrients/food
- Food security
  - Assess to enough food

Malnutrition in the U.S.

Prevalence and distribution
- Linked with economic and social factors

PREVALENCE OF FOOD INSECURITY

Key
- Below national average
- Near national average
- Above national average

Notes

Malnutrition in the U.S.: Groups at Risk

- Working poor
  - May or may not qualify for food assistance
- Isolated
  - Lack access to food resources
- Elders
  - Economic difficulties
  - Physical ailments

Malnutrition in the U.S.: Groups at Risk

- Homeless
  - Lack consistent cooking facilities
  - Limited income, if any
- Children
  - Dependent on family circumstances
  - Hunger affects school performance

Malnutrition in the U.S.

- Attacking hunger in America
  - The Food Stamp program
    - Extends food buying power
  - Special Supplemental Nutrition Program for Women, Infants, and Children (WIC)
    - Food, nutrition services for pregnant and lactating women, and children to age 5
  - National School Lunch Program
    - Free and reduced price meals
  - Child and Adult Care Food Program

Malnutrition in the Developing World

- Factors that contribute to hunger and malnutrition
  - Political disruptions and natural disasters
    - War
    - Refugees
    - Sanctions
    - Floods, droughts, mudslides, hurricanes
  - Inequitable food distribution

Notes

Malnutrition in the Developing World

- Agriculture and environment: a tricky balance
  - Environmental degradation
    - Reduced food production
    - Nutritional consequences

Malnutrition in the Developing World

- Kwashiorkor
- Marasmus

Malnutrition in the Developing World

- Iodine deficiency disorders
  - Most common cause of preventable brain damage

Notes

Malnutrition in the Developing World

- Vitamin A deficiency
  - Leading cause of preventable blindness
- Iron-deficiency anemia
  - Limits productivity of population

Malnutrition in the Developing World

- Other vitamin, mineral deficiencies
- Overweight and obesity
  - Differing cultural attitudes
  - High calorie, low nutrient dense foods